# WITH OTHERS IN YOUR ABSENCE

OTHER TITLES FROM THE EMMA PRESS

POETRY PAMPHLETS

*A warm and snouting thing*, by Ramona Herdman
*The Whimsy of Dank Ju-Ju*, by Sascha Aurora Akhtar
*Vivarium*, by Maarja Pärtna
*how the first sparks became visible*, by Simone Atangana Bekono
*do not be lulled by the dainty starlike blossom*, by Rachael Matthews

SHORT STORIES

*The Secret Box*, by Daina Tabūna
*Tiny Moons: A year of eating in Shanghai*, by Nina Mingya Powles
*Postcard Stories 2*, by Jan Carson
*Hailman*, by Leanne Radojkovich

POETRY ANTHOLOGIES

*Everything That Can Happen: Poems about the Future*
*The Emma Press Anthology of Contemporary Gothic Verse*
*The Emma Press Anthology of Illness*

BOOKS FOR CHILDREN

*Poems the wind blew in*, by Karmelo C Iribarren
*My Sneezes Are Perfect*, by Rakhshan Rizwan
*The Bee Is Not Afraid of Me: A Book of Insect Poems*
*Cloud Soup*, by Kate Wakeling

ART SQUARES

*The Goldfish*, by Ikhda Ayuning Maharsi Degoul, illustrated by Emma Wright
*Menagerie*, by Cheryl Pearson, illustrated by Amy Evans
*One day at the Taiwan Land Bank Dinosaur Museum*,

# WITH OTHERS IN YOUR ABSENCE

Poems by Zosia Kuczyńska

*For the living*

☙

by Elīna Eihmane

THE EMMA PRESS

First published in the UK in 2021 by The Emma Press Ltd.
Poems © Zosia Kuczyńska 2021.

All rights reserved.

The right of Zosia Kuczyńska to be identified as the author of this work has been asserted in accordance with the Copyright, Designs and Patents Act 1988.

ISBN 978-1-912915-83-5

A CIP catalogue record of this book is available from the British Library.

Printed and bound in the UK
by the Holodeck, Birmingham.

The Emma Press
theemmapress.com
hello@theemmapress.com
Birmingham, UK

Supported using public funding by
ARTS COUNCIL ENGLAND
LOTTERY FUNDED

# CONTENTS

| | |
|---|---:|
| 2017 | 1 |
| Here we go again | 2 |
| Jason and the Dragon's Teeth | 4 |
| He wishes for the crossing of the bar | 5 |
| I want you here so I can order breakfast | 6 |
| A Boat Lies Waiting | 7 |
| 2007 | 8 |
| Second person singular | 9 |
| Intermission | 10 |
| Poem after lines by Friedrich Schiller | 11 |
| Regeneration | 12 |
| Fifteen minutes | 13 |
| July 6 | 14 |
| Progress | 15 |
| Mandragora swallows the moon | 16 |
| *from* The golden anniversary of the thymus | 17 |
| Cliffhanger | 18 |
| The Sower | 19 |
| 'We've landed, Sarah… we've landed' | 20 |
| *Notes* | 23 |
| *Acknowledgements* | 25 |
| *About the poet* | 26 |

## *2017*

Joe and I are drinking too much Spanish lager in a bar in West Bridgford. It's been eleven months: right now I can no more elegise my dad than I could have called him 'father', and anyway 'dad' sounds flat, like it belongs in that blunt universe in which the dead can't be addressed as lyric people.

Joe reminds me that an elegy is something that you write when you've resolved your grief. I feel like an apple that's fallen from a tree into a bed of roses in winter, skewered like a severed head upon a thorny stem, which is to say I am far from resolution.

Imagine being a brain inside a jar, like Morbius, the alien war criminal who cheated death on the planet Karn. Imagine that your brain fell on the floor and lay there pulsing horribly like a winded mushroom until, with unhinged care, some space-age Victor Frankenstein picked you up and placed you safe inside a goldfish bowl.

Perched on a madcap piecemeal body, you lurch about like a wounded lobster—ungainly, ludicrous, but seeing, feeling. Imagine that my friends are patient with me; that they have offered me their ears and arms and company like Jelly Babies because I'm sad and we don't know what to do.

Back in West Bridgford I am getting teary, the way a fish gets eaten by a bird. I think I grab Joe's leg because it feels as though my ribs have detonated. Joe takes my hand and squeezes it.

# Here we go again

When I first begin to meditate, my eyes are like mandalas
weeping copious spiders from the cellar of my inability
to think of you without remembering corrugated breathing tubes.

I'm told it is perfectly natural to see monsters when I touch your things;
to be able to say what I know without being able say what's going on;
to be here one second and in the next to be in another time, another world.

I am hurtling down a tunnel shaped like the future of your absence.
Winter sun has made my outline poignant: it's like I'm being remembered,
my life with you in an obvious halo of Colour Separation Overlay.

To think of my investment in earthly matters! To think
that once I was as perkily surprised as a ripened strawberry
to find I had embraced the reality of the absurd with an open heart,

adapting to the rules of a place with a studio's limitations—
its finite corridors, its costume uniforms against which I stuck out
like a maypole in the desert—but in which I found I could be brave.

And I have been brave: I've seen you zapped with lightning, held your hand
like a second heart in mine, learned to brace myself against myself,
triangulating my limbs to strengthen my ability to watch you breathing.

And while there's life there's hope, but while there's hope there's fear:
I dreamed of miracle machines, of a bargain with which to saddle myself
like a demonic rucksack, of you waking up to ask for me by name,

by which I mean I wouldn't face the worst and was afraid.
And I am dreaming still: that this was all a dream; that you
will fall through time and space to say that you were only lost but now you're home;

that you will brush a single photogenic tear from my cheek
with a paternalistic incredulity you never had
and reassure me that you're only changing from a parent to an equal.

## *Jason and the Dragon's Teeth*

If Ray and his Hollywood gods are to be believed, you have to fight your way through whatever erupts from the teething ground before you get to enjoy a) a calm sea b) a fresh breeze and c) each other.

In other versions of the myth, however, the warriors are sown behind the Argonauts to confound their enemies as they escape. It's a matter of perspective:

are we Jason, fighting with the garden produce, against the fantastic Spring, to leave an island of sorrows? Or are we Jason, manufacturing a thousand practical and bureaucratic obstacles to overcome before loss can be apprehended?

Are we the islanders, nurturing our roses with powdered bone, setting our gardens on the unwary visitor as proof of just how well we are coping? Or are we the islanders, battling with photographs and tulip-eating squirrels, cutting down the dahlias before they're ready for it—anything that stops us seeing sails on the horizon?

Or are we Harryhausen—he who claimed (in error, I believe) that the myth required decomposing corpses and (by implication) that it's the dead that we must fight? He who made a charming and unnecessary compromise by animating bloodless skeletons?

## *He wishes for the crossing of the bar*

When this was your room you dreamed
of someone walking in, the way I do

when I dream that you walk in, the way
that anybody with a room of their own

will dream of that impossible other—
absent beloved, beloved absence, whatever—

or worse, the one who is here but not all there
walking, always walking, into the heart of it—

always wanted uninvited, always
circumventing their arrival, always

already welcomed over the threshold in
that fantasy world where only the missed can enter.

They say such simple sentences. It makes it hard to accept
that what you have wished is after all so finally impossible.

## *I want you here so I can order breakfast*

and so I see you walking down the street.

It isn't you—quite comically isn't you—but wishful thinking does a number on approaching shapes.

I think about this in the airport taxi: how clearly I have seen the sleeping giant every time I've looked towards Cave Hill, and when I wonder if I'm looking for his face it doesn't form again.

I simply won't be haunted in my life.

Back home, my room is full of summer bugs: dark moths like melanomas on the walls; flying ants; crane flies, whose other name affronts me and affronts my hate of them.

And yes, I am both furious and skittish, appalled at everything I've crushed with tissues, leaving iodine brush strokes on the bath, terrified to leave my ears uncovered in case some poison thing should get inside (which is, I hear, how someone's father died).

# *A Boat Lies Waiting*

Polly Samson writes a lyric for her husband, David Gilmour, and a nascent song becomes an elegy for his bandmate, Richard Wright, with whom he shared a kind of unsaid musical understanding.

It begins with a similar sound and feeling to *The Endless River,* an album of material compiled as a tribute to Wright's playing, taken from sessions from Pink Floyd's penultimate album, *The Division Bell.* When Gilmour plays lap steel guitar with more than usual keening, it is in answer to a keyboard phrase that is not being played by Wright, and by this we are to understand that something has become impossible.

On the studio track, a rolling piano piece recorded long ago in Gilmour's living-room begins, complete with sounds of domestic traffic, his grownup son a baby 'squawking' like a seagull; there are seagulls; Wright's voice is sampled. Interviewed, Gilmour says 'sometimes it takes a very long time before a musical idea will present itself, and will show you what it's been covering up for all that time'.

This is the kind of haunting for which there is no remedy: the realisation that you were always already mourning; that the living room in which you are forced to listen to *The Division Bell* for months on end in 1994 contains the music you will choose for a memorial in 2017; that the elegiac was always already at your fingertips.

# *2007*

Elisabeth Sladen almost drowned on location whilst shooting *Revenge of the Cybermen* in the caves at Wookey Hole. In combat boots on a speeding motor-boat, she was Sarah Jane, survivor of umpteen cliffhangers, and this was Voga, the planet of gold (to which Cybermen are fatally allergic).

This simple stunt is harder than it looks: the lake is actually a river clear enough that it appears both still and shallow. It is neither. Its current could sweep the strongest swimmer underground like paper; this cave contains its furious molecules the way a silent body seethes with antibodies, antigens.

We have seen the boat and seen the river, those uplit rocks that pass for Vogan gold. The tour-guide walks you through those caves on his shoulders like a soldier in a war film, though after months in hospital your body is the wasted battleground.

And it was a narrow escape for Lis and you: you woke one morning with your fever gone and your mother-in-law in her William Hartnell hairpiece mothering your forehead with a tissue as though in blessing; Lis, or so they say, was rescued by the stuntman, Terry Walsh, who just adored her—pulled her from that blue and deadly clarity like something rendered beautiful with hindsight.

# *Second person singular*

David Gilmour records a setting of the famous sonnet
—the one about comparing thee—afloat upon a river.
It starts with an octave leap, then down a semitone-and-tone:
eight and six; octave, sestet—clever, but not Shakespeare.
The tune is like *twinkle twinkle little star* but slightly jumbled
and with an insistent shift to the relative minor, though not as often
as I remember when I play it back inside my head.
There's no guitar and the reverb is excessive, but I listen
obsessively all day; at the end of the day, I don't remember
the middle of the sonnet or the melody in order.
And *thee* is nondescript and impersonal and intimate,
and language is transcendent only up to a given point.
An ageing rocker is singing on a boat upon a river
and thou art gone as unused grammar in the mouths of lovers.

## *Intermission*

Here's the thing: I can't abide to read these poems sometimes. It's like when my sister painted watercolour after watercolour in her grief because she thought she had to turn it into something beautiful, only to realise that when she took them down from every available surface in her home, she felt relieved.

And I have spent three years believing this: that it's my job to find a way to frame the thing that haunts me. Art alone is not a substitute for psychotherapy, and anyone who tells you otherwise is enabling your self-destruction.

Nevertheless, I realised through my obsessive framing that something about the lyric pronoun changed for me since I spent months being full of rage at the elegiac convention of addressing the dead as 'you', which felt like being asked to throw my voice into a vacuum. In short, I'd lost a thing to be towards, and whatever it was about this 'I' that was defined by this configuration had diminished.

And though I know to say 'I am not I' is nothing new, that 'you' and 'I' are often interchangeable as lyric points of view, this is perhaps the first time I have thought 'you are not you', but rather something composite—a constellation that loses something of itself each time that one of its constituent parts is no longer a point in relation to which an 'I' is capable of navigation.

## Poem after lines by Friedrich Schiller

Where did it come from, this wind that necessitated the invention
of windows that can bend? Nobody knows
except the weather people, who could take an educated guess
as to where the wind will go, perhaps, next.

Like water from a water source you never think about,
a song pours out of you in a stranger's kitchen.
Idle curiosity returns like leaves to a battered tree
that spent the winter broadcasting the brittle intricacy of its endurance:
you find you want to ask for things again and to be answered,

and when you read a stanza in a language you don't understand
and call your friend for an off-the-cuff translation, something something
something awakes in your heart that had something slept, miraculously.

## *Regeneration*

This is the second time that we've first met.
What doesn't kill you only makes you stranger,
and you are strange and hurtful and improved
like an upcycled heirloom or a child.
Childishness becomes us: we can start
again, and being treated like a kid
becomes delicious when it's mutual.
You offer me a sweet: it's like
we've just invented empathy.

## *Fifteen minutes*

The acceptable forms of affection are:

grinning at each other from a distance
gripping your arm when stepping over corpses
not looking at each other when we're talking
playing up your skills as a catcher of rats

touching your chin with my fingertips when your cheeks are
    tracked with lava
losing my temper when people point out how quickly you are dying

being impatient with others in your absence
throwing myself into the arms of robots
reciprocating the acceptance of risk

whistling

telling you it's really good to see you
asking you whether it's really good to see me

smiling and nodding and smiling and nodding
punching you in the arm

being visibly glad to be going home with you but not too happy.

## *July 6*

The day is melting like a painted clock.
O friend of mine, this village is deserted
except for all those imitation people,
and even money seems as fresh as toothpaste
in your company. How proud I am
to pay attention to your likes and dislikes,
your aversion to ginger pop. I feel as though
today is all our yesterdays, tomorrows;
that nothing had changed hands before we changed
our silver for soft drinks; that nothing
in the universe could reproduce
your not wearing a scarf. When we go back
to where the coins are dirty, let me take
you home again; let's dawdle brazenly.

## *Progress*

I dreamed that I saw nothing everywhere.
You led me through a place we didn't know
to a place we barely knew; I trusted you
because you handled me with gentleness
like the first time serious children handle pets.

Afterwards, the nightmares came and went:
the patchwork fragments of the undigested
horrors I'd accumulated, stitched
together like a suture-puckered body;
I dreamed I saw an operating table
on which the dead were resurrected wrong.

After that, the world accordioned
somewhat; buckled into flights of stairs,
and at their foot you scooped me up like Liz
Lavenza—Mrs. Frankenstein to be—
laying out tomorrow's wedding dress
as though it weren't a pointless exercise.

And you were there and you were there and you
were there, and all the people that you've been;
I woke up and it wasn't just a dream
but I told you all about it anyway.

## Mandragora swallows the moon

Let's be niche in laughter, you and I, and dress up in the face of danger
in flagrant violation of our horoscopes, whose courtly nonsense bossed our ancestors:

'Women and queers beware the orange tree', et cetera. What else is new?
To accept as fate what happens to you when you walk alone is nothing radical, Aquarius.

How's this for alterity—that I eclipse the love that stirs in you
for shirts you'll never wear again, for the past in all its rediscovered rooms;

that I have made myself at home
inside your life, like finding something better to do

in a ruined church; that the alphabet makes just as little sense
when I declare it backwards as it does recited forwards;

that my stubborn love for you has nothing to do with my being a Taurus
and you don't know why you like me so much more than making all this understood.

# *from* The golden anniversary of the thymus

*after Jacques Miller*

After four weeks, the neonatally thymectomized mouse
is grafted with certain thymus lobes; two to four months later,
the now-adult mouse is given a skin graft from its donor
& a second skin graft from a mouse of a different strain.
The skin graft from the donor will be accepted; the other
will be rejected, which means, in a nutshell, our mouse
is not now immunodeficient but rather specifically tolerant of
the thymus donor's antigens & intolerant of all others.

In terms compatible with you or I, this would be like
having your capacity to love destroyed & learning from somebody else,
& afterwards only being able to love what they loved, & to reject all others,
which is not technically a deficiency but does present its own set of problems.

## *Cliffhanger*

The third time a question is asked of us
you break the silence and answer

and when I think you're not going to wish me good morning
you wish me good morning

and when the driver stops the car
you ask them why we've stopped

and when the wrong thing is being recycled
you are there to prevent it

and in the jaws of a guided tour
you ask when it'll be over

and listening to terrible music
you say the music's terrible

and getting locked out whilst moving plants
you try the other door

and finding a way to leave the house
you don't leave me behind.

# The Sower

*for Joe Lines*

You're leaving and the sky is grey and purple
against a stubbly, indeterminate yellow
in the inverse of a painting by Van Gogh
in which a sower scatters seeds against a haybale sun.
The cows are closer to the water than they had thought possible—
really, I think anything can happen.

Did I ever tell you about that awful snow globe
in which a sower cast in three dimensions
throws handfuls of lemony grain that settle and are disturbed
and settle and are disturbed and settle again,
making a travesty of his act of labour
and looking for all the world like pissed-on manna?

*In our snowglobe, the sowing farmer has escaped from the canvas
and walks across the fertile land as a 3D printed farmer.
Give The Sower a shake and watch how the golden yellow seeds
swirl through the air and land on the fertile soil.*

I am going to believe this, hard, for all of us
because it is the best that I can do:
believe that out of this marketplace of nightmares
we might yet grow a wheat field in a snow globe—
in other words, that anything can happen.

The train is threading shards of coast together;
the birds notate their plainchant on the wires.
The sea, too, is connective—a fact I must remember
for all that it's difficult to understand this.
I'm leaving room for you inside this canvas.

# 'We've landed, Sarah... we've landed'

I think that if you ever stopped adoring me
I'd be like a tablecloth pulled out from under
a familiar tea set, flailing in the sound
of an unfamiliar audience applauding the hand that grips me,
and so I adore you constantly, with witnesses.

Is love the same as worrying about each other?
I think so. And I've an extraordinary capacity
for worry, always wanting to jump before I'm pushed,
always afraid I'm about to overstay my welcome.
Welcome me like a dog that remembers everything,
that has heard of self-respect but doesn't know how to do it.

Sometimes you look at me with such a tenderness
I feel I have to deck myself with fairy lights
to alleviate this debt I fear I am accruing.
Sometimes I need you to confirm I haven't died
because I no longer trust my own ability
to be the centre of my spatial calculations,
the now from which I gain my sense of relative time.

If you remember me then I'll remember you.
It's time to go and reacquaint myself again
with something like reality—to live with fear
like a hand I can choose either to take or not to take,
to be my own madwoman in my own attic.
It's healthy to be sick of you occasionally,
healthy to be homesick, to want things you don't want.

I love you; you sustain me; I am going home.
Everything is strange again but that's all right.
Perhaps I'll get a dog, maybe choose a family,
stop running, start running—the possibilities
don't have to be boring, but sometimes boring is the test
of being able to whistle without becoming distracted.

There will be adventures later but not too much later.
Myself is so much more now; I will learn to be
at home with more. Until we meet again we will
not meet again. Home is either coming or going
and I am always going. Until we meet again.

## NOTES

Many of these poems are very loosely based on seasons 11–14 of the 'classic' series of *Doctor Who*. Each draws its title and imagery from a different serial: 'Here we go again' from *Planet of the Spiders* by Robert Sloman and Barry Letts; 'Regeneration' from *Robot* by Terrance Dicks; 'Fifteen minutes' from *Revenge of the Cybermen* by Gerry Davis and Robert Holmes; 'July 6' from *The Android Invasion* by Terry Nation; 'Progress' from *The Brain of Morbius* by 'Robin Bland' (Terrance Dicks and Robert Holmes); 'Mandragora swallows the moon' from *The Masque of Mandragora* by Louis Marks; 'Cliffhanger' from *The Seeds of Doom* by Robert Banks Stewart; 'We've landed, Sarah… we've landed' from *The Hand of Fear* (and elements of its production history) by Bob Baker and Dave Martin. Any resemblance to actual persons, living or dead, or actual events in these poems is coincidental.

Further instances of direct quotation are as follows:

'good to see you' (*Revenge of the Cybermen*, Episode 4)

'I am going home'; 'until we meet again' (*The Hand of Fear,* Episode 4)

'Colour Separation Overlay' (or CSO) is a term used by the BBC to denote an early form of chromakey that often produced a noticeable halo around the object or actor in the scene (an effect that was particularly pronounced in the case of Jon Pertwee's Third Doctor bouffant).

'Jason and the Dragon's Teeth' references the film *Jason and the Argonauts* (1963). The first stanza contains a punctuated quotation from the film's closing scene: 'For the moment, let them enjoy a calm sea, a fresh breeze, and each other.'

'A Boat Lies Waiting' takes its title from a song of the same name by David Gilmour with lyrics by Polly Samson from his album *Rattle That Lock* (2015). The poem also quotes from the following interview: David Gilmour, 'David Gilmour—A Boat Lies Waiting (Interview)', YouTube, 2 September 2015 <https://www.youtube.com/watch?v=05Jk0UYFO1M> [accessed 5 August 2019]. Richard Wright died aged 65 in September 2008.

'Poem after lines by Friedrich Schiller' draws on a fragment from Schiller's 'Der Graf von Habsburg' as quoted in George Steiner's *After Babel*. I am grateful to Dr Stephan Ehrig for his willingness to translate poetry on demand in times of profound boredom.

'Second person singular' refers to David Gilmour's cover of a musical setting of Shakespeare's 'Sonnet 18' by Michael Kamen. This poem was first published in *The White Review*.

'*from* The golden anniversary of the thymus' is indebted to the following article: Jacques F.A.P. Miller, 'The golden anniversary of the thymus', *Nature Reviews Immunology* 11 (July 2011): 489–495 <https://www.nature.com/articles/nri2993> [accessed 27 March 2018]. Miller discovered that the thymus—presumed to be a graveyard gland for dying lymphocytes—had an immunological function and was the site of T-cell maturation.

'Cliffhanger' was first published in *Poetry Ireland Review*.

'The Sower' references a work of the same name painted in Arles, November 1888 by Vincent van Gogh. Text in italics is taken from the description of 'Van Gogh & Klevering® Snow globe The Sower' on the van Gogh Museum Shop website <https://www.vangoghmuseumshop.com/en/home-decor/641/decoration/38321/van-gogh-klevering-snow-globe-the-sower> [accessed 12 July 2019]

## ACKNOWLEDGEMENTS

Thanks to Emma for giving my poems a home again. Thanks are also due to *The White Review, Poetry Ireland Review*, *The Tangerine*, and *The Lifeboat* in this respect.

Thanks to Joe Lines and Padraig Regan for their patient and incisive critiques on virtually every draft of every poem in the book; thanks to Manuela Moser for the timely fine-tuning.

To the friends whose support made it possible to start writing about grief and then to stop writing about grief, thank you; all the nice poems are yours. Thanks to the excellent humans of 'Robot Castle' and Railway Forge for being my family and giving me a home. Thanks to Peter Cowell for the compassion.

Thanks to my sister Halina for teaching me about the thymus, and to Joe Fryer and Darren the cat for being her family; in true millennial style, thanks to my mum for the house room when I needed it.

Thanks to my late dad, to whose insistence that his daughters share his love of 1970s sci-fi and prog rock many of these poems owe their existence.

Katherine, I promise that one of these days I'll write something about jazz and information systems and possibly tadpoles.

## ABOUT THE POET

Zosia Kuczyńska is the author of *Pisanki* (The Emma Press, 2017). Her poems have appeared in *The White Review, Poetry Ireland Review,* and *The Tangerine*; her work is also featured in the forthcoming Lifeboat anthology *Queering the Green: Post-2000 Queer Irish Poetry*. She currently lives in rural Co. Wicklow, where she spends her time writing a book on Brian Friel for Palgrave Macmillan and making things out of sticks.

## ABOUT THE EMMA PRESS

The Emma Press is an independent publishing house based in the Jewellery Quarter, Birmingham, UK. It was founded in 2012 by Emma Dai'an Wright, and specialises in poetry, short fiction and children's books.

The Emma Press has been shortlisted for the Michael Marks Award for Poetry Pamphlet Publishers in 2014, 2015, 2016, 2018, and 2020, winning in 2016.

In 2020 The Emma Press received funding from Arts Council England's Elevate programme, developed to enhance the diversity of the arts and cultural sector by strengthening the resilience of diverse-led organisations.

You can find out more about The Emma Press and buy books here:

Website: theemmapress.com
Facebook @theemmapress
Twitter: @theemmapress
Instagram: @theemmapress